LETTERS FROM CHAPEL FARM

Mary Buchan

Tim Saunders Publications

TS

Tim Saunders Publications

*To my brothers. The elder is late, the other
very much alive, two years older than me. They
both played a great part in my early life.*

CONTENTS

INTRODUCTION

One very wet day, twenty years after my mother died, I decided to open a foolscap sized box with my name on it. Inside was every single letter I had written to her from Chapel Farm. Need I say more. Also in the box were and still are, every single letter I wrote to her over the first four years of our lives as farmers.

After our marriage, Mother had moved immediately to Kenya where my brother David's wife had died in child birth. She did not return for four years.

Mary Buchan

SOWING SEED

My childhood played a great part in my desire to be free and out in the fresh air. London's green belt just licked the end of my Grandmother's long garden. Once over the park railing fence the only boundary to our freedom was a thin line drawn by a small bell rung vigorously from a bedroom window to call us home in time for meals.

The long summers of 1940 and 1941 were spent at Meadle on a farm on the western edge of the Chiltern Hills. Here I was always ready to help, always there and ready to help get the cows in for milking. While there, it became my job to collect the eggs from hens that had the freedom of a large orchard and laid where ever they had a mind to.

The summer of 1948 found me again on a farm, but this time in Scotland, west of Inverness, six miles from the shores of Loch Ness. Now 15 years old, I really was able to help when they started harvesting the oats, and took great pride in stooking the sheaves, bravely putting up with the scratches on the inside of my arms left by the sharp ends of straw. Here I experienced my first harvest tea out in the field, no food had ever tasted so good.

In summer 1950, as the end of my last term at school approached, I had to decide on a career. At the time cycling was my hobby. To find my way about I used Ordnance Survey maps, found them intriguing and read them like a book. I decided I would like to be a cartographer. The only route to this career at the time was to join the Civil Service. To take up farming never entered my head.

At the beginning of August, I set off travelling by train and bicycle, to Bridge Farm in Suffolk where my eldest brother was cowman. David had chosen farming as a career after finishing his three years National Service in the army. His girlfriend Pat was nanny to the farmer's three children. I was to be a general dogsbody, helping with the children, in the house and odd jobs on the farm.

I took to life on the farm like a duck to water. After only a few days I had mastered the art of machine milking. David was able to leave me to do it in the afternoon, leaving him free to help with the cereal harvest.

By the time I was due to return home I knew what I wanted to do. Take up farming. My mother was not best pleased. My Civil Service entry exams were booked for the end of September. Mother finally agreed that I could take up farming if I should fail these exams, and then only if I went to college. The answer was simple. I made sure I passed the geography exam but made little effort to pass the others.

Meanwhile big changes had occurred. My brother took a new job as head cowman at Woodoaks Farm, a six hundred acre farm with a much larger dairy herd. With the job came a tied cottage. His girlfriend Pat took a job at a children's home to finish her training as a nanny. As David was to be on his own, I went to share his cottage and the chores. I soon found a job at Mopes Farm, a smallholding about four miles away. I was to be assistant to the herdsman, working with a pedigree herd of Jersey cows. An easy distance for me to cycle each day.

I quickly applied to Oaklands, the Hertfordshire Institute of Agriculture, for a place the following year, and started my year's practical experience. I did eight month's with the Jersey herd, then moved to Woodoaks, working with the cereal and potato harvest.

At the end of September 1951, I became a student at Oaklands and revelled in every moment.

As the college year drew towards its close, the students were frantically searching for new jobs to go to. Those that were not, were in the lucky position of returning to family farms, returning with new knowledge and ideas.

I had to find myself a new job on a new farm. On June 23, 1952 as I searched the situations vacant columns in *Farmer and Stockbreeder* magazine, I found an advertisement for an assistant to a small pedigree Jersey herd, on a farm on the Welsh Borders. That evening I phoned, giving brief details of my work so far and the results of my year at college. Two days later I received the following letter.

Chapel Farm,
Wigmore,
Herefordshire.

24-6-52

Dear Miss Royds,
Thank you for phoning me yesterday evening. I give below further details of the post offered.
I am needing someone to assist me with the building up of my pedigree Jersey herd. The work consists of the usual dairy work, i.e. milking

(machine and hand), washing of utensils, calf rearing, cleaning out boxes etc., a few poultry and seasonal field jobs. This farm is 126 acres, situated 1 mile from Wigmore village on a good access road, with Leominster 9, Hereford 20 and Shrewsbury 31 miles away, respectively. We are slightly isolated but have all modern conveniences, including television. There are good bus services to all parts.

The herd consists of 13 milkers at present, 4 in-calf heifers and 6 calves and 1 bull (13 Jerseys, 5 Aryshires and 6 crosses). Jerseys will replace all other cows gradually. My herd average in 1950 was 960 gallons and in 1951, 885 gallons per cow in 305 days. In 1951, I was 4th in my class in Herefordshire.

Wages would be £3 per week, no board deducted, overtime paid for over 47 hours per week. Time off, half-day per week, and a weekend off every third week. Any special time off would be granted.

I would want you to live as family with my wife, self and daughter of 10.

Yours truly,

L.B.R

I replied immediately, giving further details and asking for an interview.

1-7-52

Dear Miss Royds,
    Thank you for your letter dated June 25, if

convenient to you would you travel on July 9, Wednesday?

Perhaps you would kindly let me know what time you arrive at Hereford station, where I will meet you. Also please let me know the time at Hereford of your return train. The number of my car will be EOK 510 or UJ 4705.

Yours truly,
L.B.R

I really did not fancy all that travelling by train. So as soon as I was able, I went to see Curly to tell him I had been asked to go to an interview. I knew he would help me. He was very interested and pleased for me. When I told him it was in the wilds of Herefordshire, he immediately offered to drive me there, for the interview.

Curly was the machinery lecturer, in theory and practical work. Through nuts and bolts, from using soldering irons and the arc welder we had found a lot in common, from which a strong friendship had grown.

That evening I phoned Mr R to tell him I would be coming by car.

After I had left David to start at college, he found living on his own was not much fun, so he and Pat brought their wedding day forward and were married in the November. I continued to use their home as my base.

As promised, at 7am on Wednesday, July 9, Curly called for me at the cottage. Being a beautiful mid-summer morning, Curly already had the top of his pale yellow Ford coupe folded down. I felt very excited and hardly nervous as I got in beside him. As he drew away I turned and waved goodbye to Pat.

We reached the small village of Wigmore at about 12 noon, after only the briefest of stops in Cheltenham. At the village garage I asked the way to Chapel Farm. They directed us to a narrow lane that ran straight up a long steep hill. At the top, the lane levelled for a short way then plunged down hill again in a very short distance. At the bottom there was a gateway on either side of the lane. The one on the left was damp and deeply shaded by a hazel copse. The gate on the right was set well back from the road, the track leading into a stand of huge fir trees. The banks on either side were covered in heather and gorse. The warm air hummed with the buzzing of bees and insects, and was heavy with scent from the flowers and conifers.

Curly turned the car off the road into the sun and stopped. "This looks like a good place to have our lunch," he said, giving me a reassuring smile.

"Lovely," I replied. "It can't be far to the farm now."

We were both pleased to get out of the car and stretch our legs. From the car boot he fetched a rug, which I spread out on the rough grass in front of the car. He now joined me carrying a large Quality Street tin and a Thermos flask. We had plenty of time for the picnic lunch he had said he would provide and a rest before he took me on to Chapel Farm for my interview.

That lunch was an initiation to the adult world, for I soon realised we were sharing a lunch only packed for one. This gave a new slant to the day. New emotions that had only been on the periphery of my experience came to the fore and life was evidently not as simple as I thought. This clouded my perception and I went to my interview in a daze.

Just before 2pm Curly drove me the last short distance to Chapel Farm. At the end of a long track stood the farm, facing south, sheltered on two sides by the steep hill we had driven over. Curly turned the car in the small yard and stopped. I got out, now feeling a little nervous. He was going to return to the gateway to have a nap and be ready for the long drive home.

As he drove away Mr and Mrs R came out of the farmhouse. Mr R was tall, well built, wearing brown corduroy trousers and a tweed jacket with leather elbow patches and leather bound cuffs. His hair was dark and noticeably parted in the middle. He also wore a thick moustache. Mrs R was of medium build, her dark hair worn in a page boy cut. She was wearing a simple summer dress. Introductions quickly over, they took me into the house explaining as we went that it had originally been a chapel. Sometime was then spent discussing my previous work and the references that had been provided. With some amusement, because my first employer had also been a Mr R, I was shown the bedroom, which would be mine.

Then they took me out to the farm yard where Mr R went through his methods and routines for each day. The cows were milked in a six stall milking bail; at that time, an economical and popular way of milking on small farms. Milking bails had originally been designed for use on large farms so that the cows could be milked on distant fields, to avoid the long trek back to the farm.

In one corner of the yard was the Jersey bull. I was pleased to see it in a purpose built pen and was assured that I was not expected to handle him. The small mixed herd of cows were in a field below the farmhouse.

Round the yard there stood a traditional timbered barn and the original byres empty now, but used in the winter. Also several loose boxes. Behind the barn was the rick-yard, in the middle of which stood a huge ancient oak tree. On the edge of the track to the farm stood two small hay stacks covered with tarpaulins. Out of the farmyard beyond the bull pen was a pig sty. Here was a young Wessex pig being fattened for the family's supply of ham and bacon.

As we returned to the house, Curly drove back into the yard. He sat in the car and waited for me. Mr and Mrs R were evidently pleased with me because they asked me then and there if I would like to work for them. I had liked what I had seen. The work did not seem arduous, so making a quick decision, I said I would like to take the job.

After some discussion it was agreed that I would start work on July 22. They then saw me to the car.

I did not realise that this job was going to be much harder and more exacting work than any I had done previously.

In my excitement and relief, it was not until we were on our way that I realised we had not been offered a cup of tea or refreshment of any kind.

Curly drove slowly back up the track to the lane as I relaxed and came back down to earth. He chose a different route for our journey home. Again all the towns we passed through were new to me: Bromyard, Worcester, Evesham, Broadway, Chipping Norton then across to Bicester, Aylesbury and down to High Wycombe. Here as we started the long climb up the main street, Curly slowed up, turning into a hotel, drove under the archway and parked behind it.

"Time," he said, "we had something to eat. I'm starving."

I thought for a moment and realised that I too, was very hungry. "Me to," I replied.

Before going into the dining room we took time to freshen up. My hair was much in need of a comb, after driving with the roof of the car folded down. At least I had taken the trouble to wear a skirt and blouse for the interview, so did not feel conspicuous as we went to sit down. Curly had put on his tweed jacket and combed his receding curls.

During the meal we discussed the day and I told Curly more about the interview and the work I was expected to do. I was too buoyed up to admit to any misgivings I might have. I was enjoying Curly's company and did not want to spoil the moment. I sensed our friendship had a long way to go.

Being Midsummer it was barely dark when Curly pulled up a little way from David's cottage. I leant over and kissed him on the cheek.

"What was that for?" he asked, giving me his usual laughing smile.

"To thank you for everything and especially today."

"I enjoyed the day. I hope the job goes well and I promise to write you."

I got out of the car and watched Curly drive away before going into the cottage. David and Pat were still up waiting to hear all about my interview and Chapel Farm.

Two days later I said goodbye to Pat and David. My belongings were all packed and ready to be picked up by Carter Patterson. After a week's holiday with my mother, I would be met at Shrewsbury by Mr R.

JULY

I chose to be met at Shrewsbury simply because I had never been there. Curly and I had driven through Hereford on the day of my interview. On Tuesday, July 21, Mr R was there at the station to meet me with a small pick up truck. Into the back of which he put my bicycle, the trunk and the large grip I had travelled with.

I was spellbound by the views and Mr R took pleasure in answering my questions. For many miles the road ran alongside the impressive row of hills called the Long Mynd, then through Craven Arms, a small town famous for holding very large cattle and sheep markets. Then on to Ludlow with its castle, black and white timbered buildings, a very wide street ending in the narrowest, oldest bridge I had ever been across. Now we turned on to a secondary road that rambled up and down through beautiful scenery. Finally arriving at Wigmore, where we turned up the long steep lane and down past the gateway where Curly and I had shared his packed lunch. In seconds we were driving down the track to Chapel Farm. In a neighbouring field I could see the golden brown of the Jerseys and the other cows grazing.

A new phase in my life had begun.

I wrote my first letter to my mother that

evening.

Chapel Farm
Wigmore.

Monday July 21, 1952

Arrived safely at Shrewsbury, with Mr R there to meet me. Trunk and bike both arrived safely.

Mrs R had lunch ready for us when we got in. After lunch I unpacked. I helped with the evening milking. It was good to be back at work.

The weather is lovely and the countryside around here is beautiful.

Must write to Dave.

Love to Gran.

Mary

The first few days in my new job had passed satisfactorily. Now it was Saturday evening so I sat down and wrote my second letter home.

Chapel Farm
Wigmore.

6-7-52

Thank you for your letter. I have also had one from David and one from Pat. My day's work starts at 7am and ends about 6.45pm, with roughly one to one-and-three quarter hours off during the day. They are long hours, but I work at my own pace. I have all the stock to look after and 90% of the milking to do. There are only eleven cows in milk. Mr R's methods take time. Trevor the chap working here, is out all the morning and part

13

of the afternoon with the milk round.

Mr R was very ill in the spring and is not yet allowed to do much.

I do not have a single thing to do in the house. Mrs R does everything, besides playing a fairly large part on the farm, after my hours.

Their daughter Maureen is rather amusing, we should get on very well.

Although there is running water and sanitation, a spring on the farm supplies the water. When the TV is not on we use candles to save running the generator.

The second night here, I went out shooting with Mr R and Trevor. I had four shots and got the first three rabbits.

I should be able to get £3 clear a week, my overtime paying my insurance and income tax. Overtime is anything over 47 hours.

I hope you are feeling better.
Please give my love to Gran.
Love,
Mary

Chapel Farm, as the name suggests, had once been a working chapel, with ties to Wigmore Castle and the manor. After it had fallen out of use it was converted to a living dwelling and became a farm.

On the ground floor there was the dining room. Here we ate at meal times and sat in the evenings. There were two easy chairs but I sat at the table on my usual chair. There was a window at the front looking down the farm and a small window beside the chimney breast looking east. Out of the dining room on the left there was a small sitting room. Turning left down the passage took you to the front door. To the right of the of the front door was a small room used as an office. On the northern corner was the original dairy now used as a pantry, here the sides of home killed bacon, hung. Along the back of the north side was a lean-to. Entering at the back door, there was space for hanging coats and the storage of Wellington boots. Then there was the kitchen and scullery. The cooker and the refrigerator ran on Calor Gas.

At the top of the stairs was the bathroom and bedroom I used, with its window looking south. The landing led to two small bedrooms and the main bedroom. Because it was a listed building, the area over the landing and the stairs had to be left open to leave the carvings on the beams and rafters visible.

Outside on the west end of the building was an open fronted lean-to, part of which was used as a garage for the car, a Sunbeam Talbot, and part closed off. In here stood the generator to supply the electricity. The water pump that supplied the main storage tank high in the roof of the big barn, was in the tractor shed across the yard. This water was for the farm buildings and for cooling the milk in the dairy. From the dairy it was saved and collected in a large water trough in the yard for the cows to drink and for swilling down the yard after milking.

By the end of the first week, I had learned that water for use in the house had to be pumped by hand

and I was expected to do my share. One hundred and twenty five pumps a day. If I wanted a bath it had to be three hundred pumps. The hand pump stood in the kitchen from the dining room. So there was no escaping this daily chore. As a little girl staying on the farm at Meadle, I had willingly hand pumped the water for the whole house.

As soon as Mrs R had given me my breakfast, she went out to the dairy and bottled the milk for the village milk round. When Trevor arrived it was ready for him to load onto the truck with the three churns of milk for the chocolate factory in Leominster. These he left on the churn stand beside the main road opposite the end of the lane to the farm, to be picked up by factory lorry. Mrs R was entirely responsible for washing and sterilizing the milk bottles each day.

AUGUST

Chapel Farm

4-8-52

Thank you for sending my dressing gown. I forgot to mention the food is very good and plenty of it. I can get something to eat whenever I want.

The next time I go out shooting, I will send you a rabbit. I did not have a chance while Jon was here. We had a jolly good weekend, although we got a bit wet.

Mr R gave me yesterday afternoon off.

The first weekend in August was a bank holiday. My brother Jon travelled from Uxbridge on his motorbike, an old BSA. He arrived late on the Saturday afternoon just as I was finishing the milking. With advice from Mr R he went back to the village and booked into the Compasses Inn for two nights. That evening we went to Ludlow with me riding pillion. After a quick look round we had supper at The Feathers, one of the famous black and white timbered buildings in the town. Unfortunately, when we came out it was raining heavily and we both got very wet.

Next day Jon called for me at about 12 noon. We set off for the afternoon not really knowing what to do or where to go. In the village we spotted a poster advertising a motorbike scramble, something we both had an interest in. It was being held at Richards Castle, not too far away through the lanes amongst the hills. We finished the day with dinner in Hereford at The Imperial Hotel.

I never had the opportunity to go shooting in the dark by car headlamps again, though Mr R did let me wander round the farm in the evenings with the 4.10 single barrel shotgun, the one I had used on that first exciting night.

Chapel Farm

17-8-52

Thank you for your letter. Let me know the answer to Pat and David as soon as possible, for if they are rushed off to Africa I shall want to see them. I am okay for getting time off as I am not taking my weekends off. I am earning and saving, £4-10s this week. It is also okay for me to have a dog as long as it is a dog. At the moment there are three adult dogs, and one little puppy arrived yesterday. Son of Muffin the spaniel.

Alan who helps on the farm is the only person I have met of my own age. As soon as I can, I intend joining the nearest Young Farmers Club. Alan is a long distance runner.

We had a thunder storm on Friday, the rain was very, very heavy.

We have had two cows with cut teats and udders within a fortnight. Worse than those David had the other day. But cuts that will heal.

I brought my first heifer into the milking herd this week. Seems strange that she is the first, but I have not done it before. She took to the machines well, and is going to do well. Her mother has 1,000 gal average. Unfortunately, they are not Jerseys.

I am getting on better with Mrs R. It is hard at times when Mr R is not feeling well (pretty often). It causes a strained atmosphere. I like his parents very much. I had 16/- returned on my motorbike policy as I am not using it. Curly is going to try again to sell it, when he comes back from the Continent.

How can I get my money to a bank? There is not a Westminster for miles.

Since I had started my job as herdswoman at Chapel Farm, David and Pat had decided their future lay in emigrating. David was now in the process of finalising a new career as a coffee planter in Kenya. This would mean packing up their home and leaving the farm cottage.

The dogs at Chapel Farm were two greyhounds and Muffin, the spaniel. They spent most of their time in their kennel and pen. With only one afternoon off a week, I did not have any spare time to give them. There was also an assortment of farm cats. These lived in the big barn. I did get to know them as they were always around when I was working in the yard and I gave them a dish of milk after each milking. I even took the trouble to give them all names. One young cat that followed me everywhere I called Dinard.

Mr R's parents were a friendly couple and I enjoyed what little I saw of them on their Sunday visits to the farm. Mainly because they treated me with kindly respect and made me feel as I was meant to be there. They lived not far away at Brampton Bryan. Mrs R's parents lived in Solihull. They stayed at the farm for a week in August while Maureen was on holiday from school and again during the autumn half-term.

Maureen from sheer boredom, turned out to be a nuisance, always under my feet. The cows, especially the Jerseys which had been reared more like pets, were very stubborn and slow to get in for milking. Often made more difficult by Maureen hiding up trees and behind hedges, which upset them, making them plunge about and go in the wrong direction.

The flies were my other bugbear. They drove me crazy. I had never encountered them in such masses on the other farms where I had worked. I put it down to the very sheltered position of the farm, surrounded as it was by hills covered by conifers.

Due to the long hot summer we were very short of grass. The two cows that came in injured had been pushing into the hedges and tangled themselves in the barbed wire and brambles.

On the third Saturday at the farm I celebrated my 19th birthday. I received cards and gifts from all the family and the first of many letters from Curly. He sent me a small brooch in the form of a narcissi flower. Of the rest of the day I can only remember going for a solitary walk in the evening, taking Curly's letter with me and doing a lot of day dreaming.

The following Saturday, after lunch, I cycled into Leominster for the first time. Apart from the hilly lanes on leaving the farm, a fairly level distance of nine miles, on the main road.

By the time I had wandered around the town and explored the narrow streets I was feeling fairly hungry and thirsty. I looked into one or two cafes, but I was too shy and reserved to go in on my own. As the shops were closing it was time for me to set out on the return journey. Before long I was forced by intense hunger to stop and pick some plums I spied hanging over a fence. Sweet and juicy they killed my hunger pangs and I was able to finish the ride back to the farm.

I arrived back too late for supper but was able to top up with slices of bread and jam and cups of tea. I then went up to my room with the two purchases I had made; a simple notebook in which to record each cow's calving and bulling dates and any other details like cases of mastitis or injury. The other an Ordnance Survey map of Wigmore and the surrounding area.

Chapel Farm

31-8-52

Thank you for the cheque. I received it on Friday. On Saturday afternoon I cycled into Ludlow. It is one of the loveliest towns I have ever seen. I fell in love with it when Jon and I went there in the pouring rain. It has a well-known castle, narrow streets, fortified arches, and a wizard little bridge over the River Theme. The bridge is dangerous as it is so narrow.

Ludlow is in Shropshire, well, when I got there I walked straight into a motorbike shop. I have a BSA Bantam Springer coming out to the farm tomorrow evening. I may not be able to get it for another week as I have not been able to cash your cheque yet. It is second hand at £90. I shall only be giving it a trial tomorrow evening. I will let you know how it goes. I have got about £20 in hand of my own. My bank has only given me an allowance of five pounds per month. This will be okay once I get things settled.

Just after dinner, we heard a lot of excited mooing. The cows were chasing some stray pig. They turned out to be Trevor's. They are now back where they came from.

The cry of the buzzards on our range of hills fills me with a weird feeling. A mixture of peace and good things to come. There are a pair of these great and lovely birds that fly over the farm. When I hear them I just have to stop and listen and watch their gliding up and down the hill.

I have done quite a bit of reading and we watch TV quite a lot. So we hear and see all that is going on.

I will come and see Pat and David off. But I hope to see you all before then. If I get the motorbike okay.

On August 31 on my afternoon off, I cycled to

Ludlow. I could not fail to see it as I walked from the car park where I had left my bicycle safely padlocked in a sheltered corner. The Bantam Springer was displayed in a motorcycle shop window. There it was, sturdy and compact, a gleaming sage green. It had leg guards and a small windshield. With a 125cc engine, exactly what I needed to make the long journey home on.

I knew it had to be mine. I bravely entered the shop; in a very short time it was mine. I had to pay a £20- deposit and the rest on hire purchase at £4 per month. David stood surety for me. Which looking back was a big joke because David never had a penny to spare and in a matter of weeks was emigrating to Kenya.

This time I did not hesitate to go into a cafe. I ordered baked beans on toast and a plate of cakes and a pot of tea. I devoured the lot. Before setting out on the ride back to the farm, I took the trouble to buy bananas and apples, to eat when I was peckish. Feeling as though I had really achieved something I enjoyed the hilly eight-mile ride back to the farm.

You might ask why didn't I buy myself a Mars bar or sweets? In 1952 sweets were still rationed and I had grown out of the habit of using the small amount allowed each month.

David and Pat now had their sailing date, set for the end of November. Although I was keen to see them off, I was not looking forward to actually doing it.

MARY BUCHAN

SEPTEMBER

Chapel Farm

7-9-52

The Bantam Springer is just the thing. I think it is an honest deal. It is ready for me to collect whenever I get the time. This week I had last Friday off. I cycled into Leominster and got my banking fixed. All in that respect is now okay. Thank you.

I hope that Jon has a good time in Dorset, and then can come down for a weekend. It looks as though my next weekend off is going to fall in the middle of harvest.

I had now been at Chapel Farm for a little over seven weeks, in which time I had come up against more draw backs.

The open fire in the dining room, part of an Esse range, was only lit in the summer months if the family wanted baths.

For the first few weeks the weather had been mostly hot and dry, so a cool bath occasionally was not unpleasant, if of course I had remembered to do the extra hand pumping. But as the work increased and my hours grew longer I began to long for a hot bath. So I duly did my three hundred pumps and mentioned to Mrs R that I was planning to have a bath that evening. Just the pleasurable thought of a hot bath helped the evening milking go smoothly. While having supper I glanced at the fire, it did not look very promising.

Undaunted, I eventually made my way upstairs to my room, collected clean pyjamas, a towel and one of the bath cubes Jon had given me for my birthday, and went into the bathroom. I turned on the hot tap and after a little while held my fingers under the tap. The water was just coming hot. I ran a shallow bath. Three hundred pumps only allowed for the war time recommended five inches of water. Dropping my cow smelling clothes where I stood, I stepped into the bath and sat down. The water was cold, so cold tears of disappointment sprang to my eyes. That was the last time I tried to have a bath. I became adept at having a thorough wash with a kettle of boiling water. At least it saved me the trouble of having to do the three hundred pumps again.

My other problems were even more personal. I washed my *undies* out in my washing water, then rolled them in a towel to take out most of the moisture, I then hung them on the towel rail in my bedroom to dry. A day or two later I would spread them between the sheet and blanket on my bed to air while I was asleep, making sure none were there on the day Mrs R changed the sheets... I washed my work clothes as seldom as possible, as it meant using the kitchen sink. I would hang them outside to dry and hope for the best. During my time there, the few weekends I did go home I always took a bundle of dirty clothes home with me. As with the best mothers, they were always clean and dry and ready for me when I returned to the farm. A task of love, all done without the aid of a washing machine.

My other problem was what to do with used sanitary wear. The fire was never hot enough to do a quick job of burning. If it was burning brightly there was always someone sitting beside it. My answer was to wrap them tightly in newspaper and once a month take them with me when I went to Ludlow or Leominster and dispose of them in a ladies public lavatory.

Looking back now I realise my education and information on methods of women's hygiene available were seriously lacking.

Chapel Farm

21-9-52

Thank you for the letter and the things you sent with Jon. I had just begun to need the scarf, now I have the motorbike.

It was good to have Jon here, although Wednesday afternoon was very wet. We were out stooking oats when Jon arrived. I bet we looked a sight, for Alan and Trevor were covered from head to foot with Hessian sacks. I had one round my waist under my raincoat covering my knees. However it had cleared up by the evening. We spent that evening and the following morning in Ludlow. Our beloved town. I did not think Jon was capable of expressing love for a town. He seems to like Ludlow as much as I do. I take it from Gran's letter he got back safely.

Unions, blinking things. No wonder the country is in the state it's in. All Alan ever says is, "It's against union rules." Tell old Pete that I don't blame him for not joining. Union members are nothing but a lot of sheep. I don't, as it happens, go out with Alan any more. Developed same relationship as David with Peter Johnston. Unable to work efficiently, can't have my company.

The Rs have just got back from a day out. So I was busy up to 8 o'clock.

Provided the weather holds and we get the harvest in I should be home for the weekend after next. Let you know more about it later on.

I get your letters either on a Thursday or Friday morning. Mrs R usually gives them to me as I go out to change the cows from one field to another. (Split grazing). We only get one post a day.

My brother Jon decided to come and see me so I had written and given him instructions as to where he would find us. If he turned left up the lane signposted to Lingen we would be stooking oats in a small field on the left just beyond the little bridge. He arrived very shortly after we had started, already very wet from his journey. He quickly parked up his motorbike and came to help. With four of us we made short work of the job. Mr R was going to get the cows in and prepare for milking. Jon gave me a lift back to the farm. Feeling pleased with myself and Jon, I cheerfully told them Jon had worked with us all the afternoon. All he got for his trouble was a cursory smile, not even a cup of tea was offered to him. So he left for The Compasses Inn, to book in and change into dry clothes.

As soon as I had finished the milking and changed my own clothes I would join him. By 7 o'clock the rain had stopped and we set off on our motorbikes to spend the evening in Ludlow. We treated ourselves to dinner at The Feathers. As Jon had to leave after lunch the following day I was given the rest of the morning off after I had done the milking. We went back to Ludlow and visited the castle.

The oats eventually dried out enough to be carted and stacked in the rick yard. The wheat crop, grown on a field the other side of the lane to the farm from Wigmore, was combined by a local contractor and the grain stored at one end of the big barn, in cement rendered bins. The straw was baled and built into a small rick behind the barn.

The farm cats were supposed to keep the rats and mice down, but as the weather deteriorated more mice sought shelter, often more than the cats could cope with. The home grown cereals were crushed and used for feeding the cows, with a supplementary cattle cake.

Alan was 18 years old. He had a round cheerful face with a big grin and fair floppy hair. His hobby was long distance running. To keep fit for this he would jog to work and home again. Despite this he was very lazy at work. As for going out with him, I had met with him a couple of times in the evenings after work. The first time we met at a gateway into the Wigmore Rolls forest and spent the time chatting. The other time we met at a stile on a footpath leading to Wigmore Castle. The castle stands on a hillock in the valley beside the lane to the farm. We spent a happy hour exploring the castle ruins, which in 1952 were very overgrown and neglected.

On my next afternoon off, I made the trip to Hereford on my motorbike and bought myself a crash helmet. It was white, the same design that all police motorcyclists had recently started wearing.

Curly continued to write to me each week. His letters were the high spot in my routine. They were always full of news about Oaklands and the people I knew there. They often contained amusing verse and always lots of love. He was very pleased I had bought myself a motorbike and promptly bought me membership with the RAC and a year's membership with the Ludlow Motorcycle Club. I wrote regularly to him, telling about my days and confiding to him some of the problems I was experiencing.

OCTOBER

Any letters written home in October have been lost or perhaps I never had time to write any.

Before September ended I had a spare afternoon off so I took the time to explore the farm. The stream that rose somewhere on the Wigmore Rolls ran through the entire length of the farm, never very wide or very deep. Hazel and alder trees grew along each side, arching over at the top. The stream was gravel bottomed and firm to walk on. Several times I waded all the way to where it passed under the Lingen lane. It was a very peaceful experience and gave a different perspective to the farm.

As August turned into September the bushes along side the track to the farm turned a rich silver blue, a mass of ripe sloes. I was so impressed I commented on the sloes one lunchtime to Mr and Mrs R. Mr R abruptly replied, "They are not sloes, they are blackthorn bushes."

A bit taken aback I said, "But sloes are the fruit of the blackthorn." I had unintentionally scored a point.

One sunny autumn morning I walked out to a distant field to check the dry cows and heifers. The field was mainly an out crop of rock over-hanging the stream. Grass was sparse but where there was any depth of soil, the field had turned pink. Covered with a flower I had never seen before, the sight took my breath away. At lunch time I told the Rs about them and asked what they were called. Mr R was very pleased to tell me they were autumn crocus.

With the days closing in and the weather becoming more wet and windy I was very glad to still have the clothes, which had been provided for me when I worked at Mopes Farm. I had ex-land army dungarees, green jumpers, and especially welcome a Canadian land army greatcoat. I also had a black rubberised coat found in a surplus army clothing store, it was completely waterproof and proved to be indispensable.

With the shorter daylight hours, work seemed never ending. The autumn calving had started and every 10 days or so there was an extra cow to milk and a new calf to feed.

My alarm clock was set for 6 o'clock. I allowed myself a few minutes to come to terms with the new day, then by the light of my torch, dragged on my clothes, quietly went downstairs to the kitchen and put the kettle on. I would make myself a large mug of milky tea and devour two thick slices of bread, butter and marmalade. Then I would open the backdoor to check the weather, choose the most suitable coat, pull on my Wellingtons and go out into the dark.

The Hosier milking bail stood on the concrete yard, with a small brick built dairy and engine house at one end. It was surrounded on two sides by byres, loose boxes and the old barn. The third side was made up of the bulls pen and a gate leading out to the fields and to the pigsty. There was not room for the cows to be let out forwards through the bail's lifting doors so they had to back out before the next cow could enter. There was just sufficient room between the bail and the dairy and the sloping ramp to the barn for me to squeeze through. Each cow's feed was weighed and put into round galvanised bins, then stacked ready for each milking on a trolley. This stayed between milkings just inside the barn door. Before milking I pulled the trolley part way down the ramp to where I could easily reach it. The bins, 12 inches deep and 20 inches in diameter, were strongly built and when holding a ration for a cow in full milk, were heavy. As each cow took her place and was chained in, I had to rush round the back of the bail to make sure I had the right bin for the right cow, then heave up the very heavy metal door, slide the bin under and lower the door again. Rush back, check the milking machine on the other cow. Next wash the new cow's udder, take a milk sample from each teat, then put on the milking machine. Meanwhile the other cow would have finished. Before taking off the machine the very last drop of milk had to be eased out of her udder. As soon as the machine was off the cow, I would have to remove the lid with the cluster from the bucket, hang it up, take the bucket with anything up to two gallons of milk in it into the dairy, weigh it, write down the quantity against the cow's name in the record book and tip the milk into the hopper over the cooler. Then back to the bail to replace the lid, dip the cluster in a bucket of sterilising solution and so on. With stalls for six cows and two milking units there was never time to stand and stare.

There were lighter moments which always made me laugh. Patsy the oldest Jersey cow always backed out of her stall wearing her feed bin on her head. Although amusing, I still had to find time to take it off her and take it round the back to put it on the trolley.

Once a month I had the company of the milk recorder. He would arrive at the beginning of milking to take milk samples and check the weight of the milk of the pedigree cows. His being there made a pleasant change, but we did not really have time to gossip.

With a milking bail there is little shelter from the weather. During the summer I had given the matter little thought except on the very wettest days. Now with winter approaching I was virtuallly having to do the milking out in the open, which meant wearing a lot of clothing. Also it was dark when I started in the mornings and dark before I had finished in the evenings, all done by a few light bulbs giving the wavering light of a generator.

As soon as milking was finished there were the calves to bucket feed, not a job you can hurry. Then it was back to the dairy to wash all the equipment and leave it ready for the next milking. Finally, scrubbing and washing down the yard. By now the cows were all housed at night either in the byres or in the loose boxes, with hay nets I had filled with fresh hay during the day.

My final task after each milking was to feed the pig. Now the rains had come I had to wade through deep boot sucking mud to get to his sty. Once inside I had to hang the bucket up, high out of his reach, hold him off while I turned his very heavy cast iron trough up the right way, then I had to battle with him while I poured the gruel into the trough. The trough was always upside down. How I hated that pig.

By the time I was finished in the mornings it would be about 8.30am and I was ready for breakfast. I started with cereals, followed by fried home cured bacon with a fried egg and fried bread. Home cured bacon has a special taste all of its own, no bacon since has ever tasted the same. I finished with more thick slices of bread and marmalade. After I had eaten I had just enough time to wash and brush my teeth. Then it was back outside again till lunchtime at 1 o'clock.

At the end of September my half day was moved from Saturday to Friday, it didn't really make any difference to me. The reason was so that Mr R who was frequently not well enough to help with the preparations for milking was always well enough to go and play as goal keeper for the Leominster men's hockey team.

One such Saturday, Alan returned in the afternoon with his ferrets to go rabbiting. As I had an hour to spare and I had never been ferreting I was tempted to go with him. Being completely fascinated by the sport, I lost track of time. I was reminded of what I ought to be doing by the cows mooing in a huddle at the gate to the yard. I started the afternoon milking rather late. Despite the enthusiasm of the ferrets, no rabbits were caught. When Mr and Mrs R returned from Leominster and found me still only halfway through milking, I was reprimanded like a naughty school girl. However much I had enjoyed the break from routine and the ferreting, I was the one that lost out, as I was very late in for my supper that evening.

NOVEMBER

Chapel Farm

.   *7-11-52*

I received your letter today. It does not seem possible that I shall never go inside the cottage again. In fact it will be horrible going past it along the North Orbital road.

Being my afternoon off and the motorbike still out of action and not enough time to cycle anywhere, I decided to go for a scramble over the hills. Going back in my story, the chap came to do the motorbike yesterday, but said it would have to go to the garage. Fortunately, Trevor could not take it for me this morning. Well, coming back to today, Mr R stopped me as I went to get my jacket and asked me a question or two about it. Before I knew what was happening he was having a go at it for me. I went all the way to the kale field to fetch the electric fence battery. Hey presto, it went. On inspecting my battery it was out, empty, flat. It has gone down to be charged and with luck the bike should go. Thanks to Mr R.

Anyway we will wait and see.

I had time even then to explore the part of the hill I wanted to.

This morning one of the cows came in limping. She had been horned in front of the shoulder. A wound two inches deep straight into the flesh.

The weather is still remarkably warm for the time of year, apart from the gales. Several slates were blown off last night.

David and Pat had finally received their sailing date. David was now working out his notice at Woodoaks Farm and would be moving out of the cottage at the end of the month.

I had not yet made the trip home on my motorbike. Due to my lack of know-how, I had not kept the battery topped up with distilled water, so it had dried out and lost its charge.

After having the use of a motorbike, cycling was hard work. So I spent my afternoons off, exploring round the farm.

Trevor, who helped on the farm, lived further up the lane at White House Farm with his mother and brother. He was Welsh and spoke with a very pronounced accent. He had very dark hair and moustache and very blue eyes and always wore an old RAF greatcoat tied at the waist with string, and a battered trilby on his head. Smartened up he could easily have passed as a spiv. Every time he had a tale to tell he started with the words "'tis fearful, tis fearful". Despite his morbid outlook, he was always helpful.

Snowy of course, had to be the cow that was horned. In the early 1950s dehorning was not yet in full practice. Jersey cow horns naturally curl round frontwards and do not pose a threat, but one of the crossbreeds had horns growing straight out and frequently used them.

Snowy's wound healed well, but it was one more job to be seen to each day. She was also due to calve in the next few days.

David, because of his imminent move, was looking for a home for his dog Boy. Mr R changed his mind and told me I could not have a dog. I realised it was for the best, I certainly had enough to do. Meanwhile Mr R had shot the two greyhounds because they had broken into the hen run and killed most of the hens. Unfortunately for the greyhounds they were caught in the act, so a fox could not be blamed.

One particularly dull dark November day, Mr and Mrs R went out without letting me know. I did not discover the fact until I went into the farmhouse for my lunch. There was just a note telling me my lunch was ready on a plate. Cold comfort when you are very hungry after a hard mornings work. Because they were out, it meant I would have to do all the preparations for the afternoon milking myself. Mr R usually came out and leant me a hand. It was just my luck that Snowy, their favourite cow chose this day to start calving.

Although we had covered milk fever at college, I had never experienced a case. By the time I had finished milking I was really worried about Snowy. She was down in her loose box, moaning and I was unable to make her stand up.

During the four months I had been at Chapel Farm we had not called for a vet. I did not know who their vet was, I did not have a telephone number and I had no idea where Mr R was.

All very lame excuses, but that is how it was on the day. For the first time I felt my confidence dwindling and out of my depth.

At last their car headlights swung down the track to the farm. As soon as the car stopped I told Mr R about Snowy. He immediately went into the house to phone the vet. When he came out he gave me a good ticking off. I was still feeling peeved at finding only a cold lunch and not knowing they were out, so gave as good as I got. The vet eventually arrived and quickly administered a large dose of calcium to Snowy, who in turn quickly recovered, got back on her feet and calved later that evening.

The vet was understanding and gave me some good tips on recognising the early stages of milk fever. From then on for the rest of my farming career the only cows that went down with milk fever did so at night or if they started calving early out in the field.

From that day Mr and Mrs R always told me if they were going to be out.

The next big excitement in the valley was the news that the mobile threshing team were working their way round the farms threshing the corn ricks. The team consisted of a steam traction engine that hauled the threshing drum, and a heavy horse (carthorse) pulling a shepherd's hut. In this they lived when unable to get home. They came our way on a cold clear November day. I could hear the steam whistle as they trundled their way along the lane from Lingen.

Between us and the turning to Lingen there was a steep dip, a sharp bend and then up hill again. For a while everything went quiet, then one of the men arrived at the farm to ask for help with a tractor to help pull them up the hill. At long last the cavalcade came crunching and grinding down the farm track. It was the first time I had been in close contact with a steam traction engine.

They set up in the rick-yard behind the barn, beside the ancient oak tree. The thresher was positioned next to the rick of oats. The men's terriers were freed and quickly started running round the the rick yapping excitedly.

The traction engine drove the belts which in turn drove the threshing drum. The air was soon filled with the steady whirr and thrum of the thresher, the sooty smell from the traction engine boiler and the purr of the big fly wheel, interspersed with shouts from the men as they encouraged the terriers to catch the rats and mice as they fled from the rapidly shrinking rick.

Between my jobs in the yard, I kept slipping through the barn to watch. The two men were big, burly and well weathered. One wore breeches with leather gaiters and a battered bowler hat. The other who was on the rick, wore a flat cap at a rakish angle, with string tied round his trouser legs just below the knees. This prevented any excited mice from running up inside the trouser legs. They both had red spotted handkerchiefs around their necks.

Although exciting and interesting to watch, I had done my share of helping a threshing team while I worked at Woodoaks Farm. There we had run the threshing drum from the power take-off of a large tractor. It is a very dusty, dirty job.

The next time I looked out the men were picking the last of the sheaves from amongst the large hazel faggots that formed the base of the rick. The terriers, exhausted lay on their stomachs panting, their tongues hanging out.

The threshing was finished in time for them to pack up and travel to the next farm that needed them. The usual quiet descended on the farm. The oats filled another bin in the barn and I started the afternoon milking.

Chapel Farm

21-11-52

Do you know it started snowing at 3pm yesterday? This morning at 6.30am there was four inches of snow. It looked very pretty, especially the hills. It is now thawing but not quite quick enough. I hate snow.

Alan and I have at last found out how to work in unison and we have some good fun. About a fortnight ago we had an argument and we did not speak to each other for two whole days. Couple of kids aren't we? When the weather clears up we are going rabbiting in the evenings.

Yesterday afternoon after it had been snowing for nearly 36 hours, then snowing for two hours, we were still as cheerful as though the sun was shining. As we strode down the track against the snow to get the heifers in, we laughed and talked although feeling a bit on the wet side. The subject of our merriment was the fact that we had not been paid for the previous week. What makes me tell you this is, I wonder how many other people in this country of 40 hour weeks and high wages would face life as we do. If you want to know where we are, you only have to listen and the crude notes of song which float and echo in the hills will reach your ears.

The only time when all is quiet is during milking. Or is it? We invariably find one of the cows to tease eg. Snowy (get Jon to pronounce) or Patsy. These are the foundation stones of the herd, and can stand up to anything.

My motorbike went in last Wednesday.

Much to my surprise, this morning I received a parcel from Auntie Marge. Inside was a lovely warm scarf she had knitted. Also a letter, which expressed a feeling of loneliness. I am going to write to her when I have finished this, so would you give it to her?

Regarding Christmas, I should be home Christmas Eve, providing bike and weather permit. Please keep Boxing Day free for me. Otherwise you can make a few plans.

I am going to close now as I have not washed properly for two days. It is too cold.

P.S. Would you please get for me a pair of binoculars

and give to David and Pat, with a little present for Pat of some sort or other. I will give you £5 to do this when I see you. If you can't get the glasses, would you give them the money? It sounds a lot but it is to cover David's birthday, and a parting gift for them both.

◆ ◆ ◆

I had got up as usual, and made my way out to the yard. The first to make footsteps in the deep snow, always a thrill. My first job was to go round the byres and loose boxes letting out the milking cows, who behaved as though they had been let out to grass for the first time in the spring. Despite extra layers of clothes, it was a job to keep warm and everything took much longer. Except cooling the milk.

The snow, despite the added difficulties, was exhilarating and no doubt explains the joyful feelings of Alan and myself.

Trevor, as he drove down to the farm, was the first to make tracks in the deep snow on the farm track. As soon as he was out of the cab he was telling me that the Aberystwyth Mountain Pass was closed because the snow was so deep. I had never seen or heard him so excited.

Twenty years passed before I discovered the Aberystwyth Mountain Pass for myself. On a day in early summer as I climbed the last hill out of Ryhader, the pass lay before me. I knew then why Trevor had been so excited.

The tracks he had made, made it easier for Alan

and I as we pushed the cows up the track and into the kale field. Later in the day, moving the electric fence was not so pleasant. Each time we knocked a kale plant, snow slid off a leaf into our Wellingtons.

Maureen was overjoyed, as it was impossible for her father to drive her to school that day, also as it was a Friday it gave her a long weekend to spend building snowmen.

As the weather grew colder so did the farmhouse. The only heat came from the forlorn fire in the dining room. At the end of the day, dog tired I would crawl into bed with a hot water bottle, bed socks and an old jumper round my shoulders and lie there with my teeth chattering until I fell asleep.

Much to my surprise on the morning of the snow I came into lunch and found a parcel waiting for me. It was from my Aunt Marge and the contents were a life saver. Inside the parcel was a big thick scarf roughly knitted out of remnants of wool all colours of the rainbow. About four feet long and eighteen inches wide. That night when I went to bed I wrapped it round my middle, soon got warm and slept soundly.

As it was my half-day, I took up Trevor's invitation to visit White House Farm for the first time. After lunch I wrapped up well, pulled on my Wellingtons and set off up the track to the lane and walked on to Trevor's, only about three quarters of a mile, but hard work in the snow.

The small farmhouse was set back a field's width from the road with a few low buildings huddled round a small yard. Everywhere was very quiet and as far as I could see the surrounding countryside was blanketed in snow.

I knocked on the door and as I waited, I wondered what to expect. A gentle, softly spoken, white haired lady answered the door. As soon as she realised who I was, I was quickly invited in and made very welcome. My coat was soon off and I was sat down in front of the shining black range set into an old inglenook. The door to the fire stood open and gave out a welcome warmth. In no time at all I was telling Mrs Watson all about myself and how I came to work at Chapel Farm. Before long, Jim, Trevor's older brother came in from checking his stock. He was so different to Trevor. Stockily built, with a well-weathered face full of fun. Wearing a flat cap at a jaunty angle.

All the time I had been there, the huge black kettle hanging on a chain over the fire had been singing to itself. Now, Mrs Watson swung it out on the bracket and poured a little hot water into the tea pot to warm it, swung the kettle back and lowered it on to the stove to bring it back to the boil.

By the light of oil lamps Mrs Watson spread a fresh white cloth over the kitchen table and set out plates and cutlery. We sat up to the table and tucked into homemade bread with cheese or home reared ham, scones, butter and jam. I had not felt so at home and welcome for weeks. It was late in the evening when I decided I really must leave and go back to Chapel Farm. Jim insisted on taking me back as far as the top of the farm track on his tractor.

At the back door I stamped the snow from my boots; an easy way to let them know I was back. As I was greeted in the dinning room I was gratified to find that Mr and Mrs R had been worried about me. I promised not to be so late in again but did not tell them where I had been. The next day they puzzled over whose tractor tyre marks stopped in the lane at the top of the track. The bonhomie with Alan did not last long and by the time I took four day's off to go home for David and Pat's farewell, life was back to normal.

A day or two before the snow storm, the neighbours further along the lane had killed their porker. We had all heard his frantic squeals echo round the hills as they slit his throat.

This reminded Mr and Mrs R that time was running out for their pig and he became a topic of conversation. I suddenly had visions of a fresh pink carcass being black and blue. It was time to stop kicking the pig.

Because my motorbike was in Ludlow being repaired and there was still a lot of snow about, I travelled home by bus and train. Trevor gave me a lift down to the bus stop in Wigmore where I caught the bus to Hereford, then the train to Paddington and the Metropolitan line out to Uxbridge. From the station it was a walk of about two miles to my grandmother's house.

The little I can remember of the saddest few days in my life is on the Monday I went to Tilbury docks with David.

He took with him the last of their luggage, so they would not have to carry it on their last morning. London was already lost in a thick fog. Of Tilbury I can only remember the vast sides of a huge ship, and of feeling miserable and cold. David had hoped he would be able to show me their cabin, but they did not allow him to take me on board.

On the day they were to embark, David, Pat, Jon and I left our gran's house early in the morning, walking down to Uxbridge Metropoliton station. Mother was unable to leave our grandmother. We boarded the train, Jon and I sitting opposite David and Pat. Cheerful conversation soon ended, tears just below the surface preventing us from talking. As the train neared Baker Street, I stood up and bade them a silent farewell. I had to leave them and make my way to Paddington and my return to Wigmore. Jon continued with them, to see them onto the liner, then to his job in the city. I had never felt so bereft.

At long last the bus dropped me at Wigmore, as it was still light, I trudged my weary way up the lane and back to Chapel Farm.

Two days later I developed a really awful cold but struggled on. To keep myself going I carried a hip flask of Boots the Chemist's Influenza Mixture and kept taking a swig from it. I have no idea what it contained but it certainly helped. I did not get any sympathy or comfort from Mr and Mrs R. At least work went back to normal as the snow gradually disappeared.

My one great relief was finding, while I was away, the pig had gone to be slaughtered at the local bacon factory. A couple of days of having to wade through deep mud and wrestle with the pig had quickly sealed his fate. For the first time they had not followed the local tradition of having him killed on the farm. Even so for the next couple of weeks we lived on fresh pork and sausages. New sides of bacon were soon hanging in the pantry.

Wigmore village is situated on the edge of a very low lying area. I had been told that it flooded every winter, ideal for wild geese and ducks to spend the winter there. I had seen and heard, while out on the farm, skeins of geese and wildfowl flying in that direction. Now the local farmers including Mr R occasionally gathered for a day's shooting. Resulting in roast duck or pheasant as a change for Sunday lunch.

DECEMBER

Chapel Farm

12-12-52

My cold is almost gone and I feel a lot better. The snow has completely gone. But they say there is going to be some more. We have just had three of the mildest days possible, however it is going to freeze tonight.

I had a letter from David today, he wrote it last Sunday while they were waiting for the fog to lift. He said he was wearing the shirt I gave him for his birthday.

Today is also my half day, so I cycled to Leintwardine, left my bicycle at the garage (to pick up later). Caught the bus to Ludlow, did some shopping, had some tea and collected my motorbike and returned to the farm on it. I had another tea when I got in.

The motorbike is going, as far as I know, quite well. If the weather is mild at Christmas, I shall come home on it.

I feel much happier and everything seems a little more friendly. Alan annoys me intensely. Haven't spoken to him for two days. He is so stupidly childish. What I should say is he won't speak to me. He is lazy and too rough with the cows, also annoyed because I won't go out with him.

The bus journey this afternoon showed me a bit more of Shropshire. I think it is one of the loveliest counties I have ever been in.

David and Pat's departure for Kenya was held up for four days by the worst fog London had ever experienced. Their liner had to sit in The Thames and wait for it to clear.

At the same time as collecting my motorbike I had bought myself a proper motorbike coat and over trousers.

On my next afternoon off I caught the bus to Leintwardine, reclaimed my bicycle from the repair garage and cycled back to the farm.

With the short daylight hours and long days of work, the days to my next weekend off and Christmas, soon passed. Christmas Eve fell on the Wednesday that year. Although I was starting a five day break I was still expected to do the morning milking before I left. So keen was I to get on my way that I just flew through the work. This did not go un-noticed. As I ran into the house Mr R remarked, "That was quick. Why can't you do that every day?"

As soon as lunch was over, I set out on the long journey home on my motorbike, for the first time. A distance of about 140 miles. On the pillion I had my weekend grip and my usual bundle of used sanitary wear for disposal. I made my first stop in Bromyard and parked up outside the public lavatories. With my bundle I walked into the Ladies, much to the surprise of a lady coming out. In a severe voice she said, "Shouldn't you be next door?"

"No," I replied, smugly, completely innocent, and continued on my way. She had mistaken me for a man, dressed as I was in all my new motorcycle clothes and crash helmet.

I was soon back on the road, using the same route Curly and I had taken back in July. I made my next stop in Chipping Norton. Here it was easy to park and the public conveniences were situated in the old market building in the middle of the town.

By the time I reached Aylesbury, it was very misty and getting dark. I was also having trouble changing gear. As luck would have it, a set of traffic lights stopped me right outside a garage, so I wheeled my bike in and asked for their help. As soon as they realised I was a girl, help was quickly given, the problem quickly solved. Refusing my offer of payment, I thanked them and set off again for Uxbridge, finally arriving at my gran's house at about 6 o'clock. Mum, Jon and Gran were very pleased to see me.

Without David and Pat, Christmas was very quiet. Leaving Jon to mind Gran, I went to the early church service with Mother. During the day Jon and I amused ourselves playing table tennis on the dining room table, as we used to when at school.

Jon had arrived home from work on the Christmas eve with a good selection of bottles. Mother ticked him off for encouraging me to drink (one Martini).

I had promised myself that on Boxing Day I

would go and seek out Curly. The steady stream of letters from him had never ceased. He had over the months also sent me two books, The Bullet in the Ballet by Carl Brahms and SJ Simon. Also Precious Bane by Mary Webb.

The weather had deteriorated over night and everything was shrouded in thick freezing fog. Not deterred, I dressed in all my gear and set out on my motorbike for St Albans. Although it was Boxing Day, I was convinced Curly would be in his usual place at college. After only a few miles I was frozen stiff and had to keep wiping the frozen fog off my goggles.

Reaching Oaklands I drove slowly up the drive, and had my first misgivings. With the thick fog it was very eerie under the huge bare trees their branches hanging with frozen fog, and it was so quiet. There was not a soul to be seen. As I passed the cattle yard the familiar sounds and smells gave me a little hope, so I went on to the Machinery Workshop, stopped, turned off the engine and for a minute or two just sat. Frightened to make a noise I quietly pulled the bike up onto its stand. Then with a hand stiff in its leather gauntlet turned the handle of the door to the workshop and gave the door a push, to my surprise and relief it opened. I poked my head in and peered across the interior to the corner where the little office was, to my delight the light was on. Gently closing the door, I silently made my way between the farm machinery waiting for students to work on when the new term started. Now trembling with cold, anxiety and emotion, I knocked on the office door. Through the grubby window I saw Curly rise from his seat, then the door opened and a very surprised Curly took me in his arms and gave me a big hug.

As pleased to see me as I was him, he quickly explained he had to go to some friends for Christmas drinks, but he would get back as soon as he could. While he made me a pot of tea, I took off my now thawing coat and hung it to dry near the oil stove that was giving off a cosy heat. Before he left, he wheeled my bike into the workshop to keep it dry.

After what seemed like a life time, he returned. Now well past lunchtime he told me he knew where we could go to get something to eat. While Curly turned out the stove, I put my now warm damp coat back on and we went out, got into his car and set off through the fog. Curly eventually pulled into the car park of the Busy Bee Road Transport Cafe. As it was Boxing Day it was very quiet. The only customers were lorry drivers who took no notice of us. Both of us being very hungry we chose the mixed grill with chips and bread and butter with a large pot of tea. We had a lot of catching up to do, but our time together ran out. He was expected home, and I had to go onto visit other friends, the official reason for my trip to St Albans. I stayed the night with them and returned to Uxbridge the next day.

Chapel Farm

29-12-52

I arrived back safely after an uneventful journey. It was however rather damp until just before Chipping Norton, where I stopped and had a cup of coffee. The cheapest and best I had ever had (4d). I stopped in Evesham for something to eat. I got in just after 3.30 pm and started work at 4pm.

Another cow has calved but not Carissima. Please thank Gran for me. I enjoyed being with you all and the complete freedom of being at home.

JANUARY

Chapel Farm

6-1-53

Thank you for your letter, which I received this morning. I did not write as I was expecting to hear from you. Since I have been back I have not stopped working. We have been baling hay, three cows calved which means three more to milk.

I still get up at 6am but start at 6.30am. Excluding today it has been 7.30pm before I finish in the evenings. So this morning at breakfast Mr R decided to give me an extra half-day per week.

So now I get two half days a week, Wednesday and Friday afternoons. We also start working earlier in the afternoon.

The pyjamas are very comfortable and warm. I am sleeping more soundly at night.

The weather has been warm, cold, freezing 14 degs Fahr and very sunny in between. We have not had any snow. I saw on the TV news reel that London had got it.

Last Sunday I took Maureen for a walk. She was thrilled.

I spent the next few days settling back to work. Helping newly calved cows fit back into the milking herd and teaching their calves to drink from a bucket. This could sometimes be difficult especially if the calf was very obstinate. One day as I struggled I remembered the method I had been shown as an 8 year old, while on holiday at Meadle Farm. Despite the extra work, there was something very satisfying about feeding a young calf, standing astride their warm excited bodies, with two fingers being strongly sucked as you lowered your hand into the warm milk, often having to put up with bruised knuckles when they butted your hand hard against the side of the bucket.

As with the threshing, a contractor would visit the small farms with a stationary baler so that the hay in ricks could be baled. This meant I did not have to wait for Trevor to cut the hay from the rick each day. The hay bales were so much easier to handle, and as many as possible were stacked in the barn. While the baler was on the farm they also baled the oat straw left from the threshing.

To be given an extra half day off was bliss, even though I was never able to have a lie in. This meant I was able to go into Leominster or Ludlow one afternoon and go exploring round the farm the other afternoon.

Starting milking earlier in the afternoon was not really much help, for it meant I had to finish all the odd jobs earlier. Before I started the milking I did have time to go into the farmhouse for a cup of tea and something to eat.

As I had worked through the new year without a break I was given a couple of hours off, so I asked Maureen if she would like to accompany me on one of my walks.

It was the first time she had gone beyond the home fields into the woods on the hill above the farm. When not at school she was left very much to her own devices. She occasionally came out to the yard and spent some time with Beauty, Snowy's first heifer calf, now a yearling. Maureen was training her to walk on the halter.

Chapel farm.

14-1-53

Thank you for your letter, which I received this morning. Yesterday I received from Auntie a pair of tarred wool mittens. Just what I needed. I was going to try and knit some for myself.

I had a quick cold just after I got back. The only comment was "I can tell you've been home".

It is good fun with the extra time off. I was off this afternoon. As the weather was so pleasant I thought I would explore a bit more of the neighbouring countryside. So I set off on my two feet and covered about four miles of new and lovely countryside.

I was talking to Trevor this morning and he told me to call on Mrs Davies, our nearest neighbour. I said I would. So I dropped in on the way back. Mr Davies has about 30 acres of grass on which he raises four or five calves a year to 12 months, then sells them on as stores. He and she are both of farming stock and once owned a larger farm near Ludlow. I suppose you could call him retired. He is however scared stiff of milking a cow. I spent two pleasant hours chatting with them and had a

*light tea. I can go up there any time I like, so I expect I
will go up there quite a bit. It will mean seeing more of
Trevor, but I can handle him okay. Their house is about
three hundred years old, very small, no water and no
lights except of course for paraffin lamps.*

*As nothing else of interest has happened, I will close
to you and write a short note to Jon.*

*Please make a booking for me at Muriel Seldon's, to
have a semi shingle on Saturday morning February 14.
I can't manage curls out here.*

Apart from my visit to the Watsons at White House
Farm while I had been snowbound in November, I
had not had time to visit other neighbours. Trevor
had on several occasions told me that I was very
welcome to call in for a cup of tea with them. I had
spoken to them out on the lane, meeting them as
they walked home from trips into local towns on
the bus. Now with extra time off I had time to spare
so with a reminder from Trevor, I had visited the
Davies. Trevor as the local odd job man, milked their
house cow each day for them.

During my last term at Oaklands I had my hair
cut and finished in a bubble cut perm. Now the perm
was grown out and too long. I wanted to look my
best at the reunion. The Oaklands reunion was being
organised by the 51-52 year students for February
14, for which I had booked a long weekend off. We
were all meeting for a meal, then onto a show, Kiss

me Kate, in London.

Chapel Farm

22-1-53

I am so excited, I hardly know what I am doing. Things down here began to get a bit stiff again, with the result that I found the answer to my growing bad temper, which was invariably lost on the animals. In fact, I rather shocked myself when I went for one of the calves. I knew then that something had got to be done. So I did. I wrote to the Relief Herdswoman Service in Suffolk. I posted it yesterday. They got it this morning and telephoned me. I phoned them a few minutes ago. A young man answered and he seemed pleased with me, from my letter. They need us quite desperately as the service is expanding everyday. I am now waiting for him to write with further particulars. Then I shall write giving the day I can go for an interview. I told him it would not be until February 14. This he did not mind.

The reason I can't do anything immediately is the last half of the answer that I found to be the reason for the change in my character, which I think I've stopped.

As you know Alan and I couldn't get on. In fact he made me boil. He has been the cause of half the trouble. However, about a fortnight ago he hurt his foot. To get out of work he went on the panel. Last Monday he started work again. He would do nothing unless I asked him to. I decided then and there that either he went or I did. Tuesday morning he did nothing in 3/4 hour except milk Kitty. He only started to work when Mrs R came out. That did it, I just boiled over and told him just what

I thought of him in no uncertain words.

At breakfast time Mr R asked the usual question. "Why did milking take so long?" I told him the answer. "I did it single handed while Alan stood and watched." He shot up from the table. EXIT Alan has now got the sack. This means we are understaffed with plenty of work to do. So you see I don't really want to leave them in the lurch at the moment. But I think this new job is the realisation of my ambition, it is too good to let it slip.

It sounds a super job, travelling all over the British Isles. Please give me your views on the last paragraph, as I don't really know what to do. I do think though that Mr R will understand if I tell him it is the job I have been waiting for.

At the moment I have little else to say. Except I did not expect things to move so quickly.

This last letter is self-explanatory and there is nothing to add.

FEBRUARY

The next letter I addressed as The Hermits Hole.

The Hermits Hole,
Wigmore.

2-2-53

Thank you for your letter. There is little more I can say at the moment regarding the job, for I have not had a reply. Although I shall, I hope be able to get home more often, I do not want, if I can help it, to live in Uxbridge again. It would drive me crazy.

Regarding my motorbike I intend paying off the hire purchase before the end of this month. It will leave me with £10 or £15 capital in the bank. But all the while it is on HP I don't own the money in the bank or the bike.

Still on the subject of motorbikes, Curly has found a purchaser for the Corgi. We have started our own hire purchase firm. The lad buying it is paying £25, £5 deposit and £2 per month. I received the deposit and first instalment today.

Regarding this place, I have learnt a lot from Trevor, regarding Mr and Mrs R and several of my own suspicions have been confirmed. I am leaving for certain whatever the job. I shall not write these interesting things to you here. You will have to wait until I see you. A new man came for an interview today. That is all I know.

We had a few mild days, ending in short blizzards on Saturday, which did not settle.

Will write again as soon as I hear anything.

My weekend off arrived and setting out on the Friday afternoon I made the long trip to Uxbridge. It was lovely to be home. I went to bed early, after a long hot bath and slept soundly.

Next morning Saturday the 14th was the day of the reunion. I had my hair cut, it felt good and I felt more confident. It would be very easy to keep clean and never really looked untidy. I was looking forward to the reunion, not only to meet up again with the other students of my year but because the boys organising the reunion had unwittingly invited Curly. I was to make my own way to the rendezvous. Curly had written saying he would take me home afterwards.

We did not sit next to each other at the meal, but with a lot of cunning, managed to sit next to each other in the theatre. At the end of the performance after making our farewells, we slipped out together, to where his car was parked. He drove me back to Uxbridge and stopped a good way short of Gran's house, as we had some serious catching up to do. We eventually parted and in a dream I made my way home to an anxious mother and my bed.

The following morning I had a consultation with Mum and Jon and we decided it was definitely time for me to find other work and to leave Chapel Farm.

Jon and I spent Sunday on our motorbikes calling on all the local farms, with me asking for work. We ended up back at Woodoaks Farm, Maple Cross where David had been herdsman and I had worked for three months before starting college.

Mr Findlay, despite his reputation for being a hard man and exacting boss, was pleased to see me and gave me a job working with the milking team that managed his pedigree Ayrshire dairy herd.

I would start work in a little over a month's time and decided to give Mr R four week's notice. With Jon and Mum's help, I wrote a very succinct letter of resignation, which I gave to him when I returned to the farm on the Monday evening.

I did not try to pursue the job with the Relief Herdswoman Service again, it would be easier to do when I was working for Mr Findlay.

My first motorbike was a motor scooter called a Corgi. It had a maximum speed of 30mph and was ideal for short trips and had been great fun. I had used it to go home for weekends while I was at Oaklands.

As I got to know Trevor and his brother Jim, I learned more about Mr and Mrs R and how they were unable to keep a herdsperson for more than a few months. Prior to me they had had an ex-land army girl.

The day was bright and dry but very cold. My journey back to the farm went well until just before reaching Evesham. The engine started stuttering and finally stopped. I immediately checked the tank for petrol, but there was plenty there. So I sat on the bike, considered my options and had a look around. I was on a straight main road with no housing and very little traffic. However, a little way ahead I could see some men working on the side of the road. They had a small truck. Without hesitating I dismounted and pushed the bike till I reached them. They stopped work and leant on their shovels while I explained my predicament and asked for their help. As when I broke down in Aylesbury, as soon as they realised I was a girl, they could not do enough for me. They hefted the bike into the back of the truck, made room for me in the cab and drove me to the next garage along the road. I thanked them and they returned to their job tidying the roadside. Luckily the problem was minor and did not take long to put right. For the small charge of a half crown, I was on my way again.

Mr R's reaction on receiving my letter of notice, was to complain that it did not give him long to find someone else. With the relief of knowing I was leaving, I felt very bold and shut him up, saying he was lucky to have four weeks, pointing out, as I was paid weekly, I need only have given him a week's notice.

The atmosphere grew even more chilly so when not at work I spent more time visiting the Watsons.

Chapel Farm

.   *27-2-53*

Sorry I have not written before. We are still short of labour but I am enjoying the work. I haven't done anything about packing yet.

Yesterday was my half day. As it was a glorious day I went to Knighton, a very interesting market town. I came back and had tea with the Watsons. I like them more and more. I went out with Jim in the evening.

Sorry this is short. I want to post it this evening, then go up to the Watsons for an hour.

Chapel Farm

28-2-53

Here is the letter I promised   you. I went down to the village and posted the last one, then I went up to the White House and spent a pleasant hour with Mrs Watson. Mr and Mrs R would love to know where I go. So far all their guesses have been wrong.

We all think it best that they do not know, unless they ask me outright. At the moment they are pumping Trevor, but Trev won't be pumped. One of their wild guesses is that I go down to Alan's place in the village. They have got someone to take my place but have not told me yet.

I am still working the same long hours but enjoy it, knowing I am free. We have also been having some lovely weather. Today has been very misty.

Going back to the Watsons, for they are the only people I know down here. I shall be going up there quite a bit in these last few weeks. Next Wednesday Jim is taking me out again. First we are going to Knighton and then up country to show me some of Wales. Jim is a jolly chap and not a bit like Trevor.

There is not much else to say. Will tell you everything else when I see you. Will write at the end of the week.

Going out with Jim was a further experience of learning about life. When we stopped in a town he always made straight for his favourite hostelry, in all of these he was well-known. I became an expert in making a glass of sweet cider last a long time. Before returning home he would stop his car in some remote place fully expecting some cuddling and kissing. Not satisfied with this he always asked for more. Despite a serious lack of informed knowledge on the facts of life I knew when to say "No."

MARCH

The last letter.

Chapel Farm

6-3-53

I hope you got my letters okay. You won't get this until Monday although I'm writing it tonight, which is Friday. Since I last wrote, I have spent Monday evening with Mrs Watson and Jim.

Wednesday afternoon was mine and as I told you, Jim was taking me out. We set out at 3.15pm. It was a lovely afternoon. We went to Presteigne, Cascob, New Radnor, Walton, Kington, Presteigne and home.

Cascob is where Jim's father had, when he was alive, a three hundred acre farm. We also passed two large farms, which are owned by two of his uncles. I expect I shall go to the White House to see them tomorrow evening.

At the moment Mr R has a poisoned hand. It was 8 o'clock before I finished this evening. The weather is most peculiar. We get wonderful sun during the day and heavy fog at night. Jim and I were caught in it yesterday evening.

I still have done nothing about packing. I will however be with you next Saturday evening sometime. My push bike may reach you before anything else so don't think the others have been mislaid.

To my surprise, at the end of our last afternoon we spent out together, Jim asked me to marry him. He told me I was the only girl to say *no* to his further demands, and he admired me for it.

I was to say, at the very least, very surprised. Before giving him an answer I took time to imagine myself married to a small time farmer, a good bit older than me, on a remote farm on the Welsh Borders. However much I wanted to be a farmer, I knew it was not the right time or place for me. I said, "I'm sorry Jim, I'm not ready for marriage and my new job beckons."

I eventually had time to do my packing and arranged for my trunk and bicycle to be picked up by Carter Patterson and eventually delivered to Uxbridge.

Despite the difficulties of working for Mr and Mrs R I was saddened to leave. I had become very fond of the cows and their calves. Apart from the mishap with Snowy, I had done my best with a difficult job. I always managed to be one step in front of Mr R when it came to which cow was ready to be served and those that had slipped service and when. One day he had queried me on my information about a certain cow. I told him I had been keeping my own herd records, recording everything that happened with every cow. He was surprised and gave me rare words of approval.

I loved the countryside around the farm and the wildness of the whole area. I would really miss my airborne companions, the beautiful buzzards. To this day their call is imprinted on my soul. I have only to hear one note and I know if I look up I will eventually see a soaring bird high in the sky.

On Saturday, March 13 after doing the morning milking for the last time, I was given my last pay packet and Mrs R returned my ration book to me. After my last lunch with them and Maureen, I strapped my remaining possessions onto the pillion of my motorbike and set off up the farm track for the last time on the long journey home.

THE SOWN SEED RIPENED TO BE RESOWN

I took up my new job at Woodoaks Farm the following Monday making the seven mile journey from Uxbridge to Maple Cross on my motorbike.

I started work at 8am and finished at 5pm with alternate Saturdays and Sundays off. I worked in a weekend milking team, which meant being on the job at 5am. For all this I was paid £3 a week. Because of the early hours of weekend work I needed to find digs near to the job as soon as possible. As I was in the lucky position of knowing most of the men working on the farm from when I lived with David in his cottage, I asked around and soon found digs with George and Yvonne Fuel. George was head tractor driver and had worked on the farm since he left school when he was 14 years old.

They had three small boys, the youngest still a toddler. Their cottage was more modern and slightly larger than the one I had shared with David. They gave me the smallest bedroom for £1 per week. I took on the daily task of ironing the boys' clothes and washing up after the evening meal.

My friendship with Curly grew and we were soon seeing each other once or twice a week.

Then one evening the motorbike seized up on me with a loud bang just as I was starting it to return to Maple Cross after spending the evening with Mum, Gran and Jon. Jon gave me a lift back to the farm that night and the next time I saw Curly I asked him if he could spare the time to diagnose the problem for me.

On May 1, 1953 he picked me up at Maple Cross and took me to Uxbridge. By now I knew I was falling in love with Curly, and I had some problems to face. When I introduced him to my mother I would have liked to introduce him as my boyfriend, but knew it was out of the question. Curly was married, 15 years my senior and a Roman Catholic. I was not yet 21 years old and what my mother said, was law to me. She would have been horrified.

So I introduced him as the friend and help he had been. She was pleased to meet him as she had over the last two years heard a lot about him from myself and Jon. We had been supporting him for some time as fans at his motorbike scrambles.

With Jon to help him, they dismantled my bike and found a piston ring had broken and jammed the piston. It would mean a new engine.

While they worked on the bike, I had the time to think about my future and came to the conclusion that I would never have a future with Curly. By the time we arrived back at Maple Cross I had made up my mind. I knew I had to stop seeing him. Not at all what I'd had in mind while I waited for him to pick me up earlier in the evening.

As usual after we had been out Curly pulled up under the Scots pines at the entrance to Woodoaks Farm. I allowed myself the pleasure for one last time of kissing, cuddling and chatting with him. Above us the may bugs were performing their clumsy courting flights. Occasionally one would land on the car with a thud and slide to the ground.

At last it was time to thank Curly for his help. As usual he said it was nothing and he would do anything for me. As he tried to kiss me good night, I held him off and told him it was all over, I could not go on seeing him. He sat back and looked me straight in the eye and he knew I meant. We parted as friends.

The following few weeks were the worst. I went around in a numb daze, trying to blot out all thoughts of him from my mind by concentrating on my job. Several times Jon asked me to accompany him to see Curly as we had been in the habit of doing. Each time I had to find a reasonable excuse for not going.

Fortunately time heals, I was during the day working with four or five young men, all of whom were great wags in their own eyes. It was difficult not to laugh at, and with them.

A light began to shine at the end of my long dark tunnel, and there was to be a Coronation.

THE RAINBOW

The rainbow's arch caresses land
where yesterday, exactly there
I had stood and looked around.

Overawed by all I saw
that widespread tranquil scene,
in every shade of brown and green.

On each sweet breath of air
bird song the only sound to hear.

I wish I was there now
to see my world, through
those brightly coloured bands.

Mary Buchan
2017

ABOUT THE AUTHOR

When Mary left school she went straight into farming. Her first job was as a herdswoman on a small isolated farm on the English/Welsh border at Wigmore. When she married, she rented a farm with her husband. While bringing up their  two daughters and son, Mary became a professional upholsterer. In 1997 she joined a writing group and discovered that she prefers poetry to prose. "I only write when I am seriously moved," reveals Mary from Marnhull, Dorset.

OTHER TITLES
featuring Mary's poetry

The Westcountry Collection
Hope for Ukraine

from Tim Saunders Publications
tsaunderspubs.weebly.com

THE PAUL CAVE PRIZE FOR LITERATURE

What we are looking for

All forms of poetry: haiku, free verse, sonnet, acrostic, villanelle, ballad, limerick, ode, elegy, flash fiction, short stories and novellas. Work must be new and unpublished. International submissions welcome.

Guidelines

Poems
should not exceed 30 lines

Flash fiction
should not exceed 300 words

Short stories
should not exceed 1,000 words

Novellas
should not exceed 10,000 words

Prizes

Best Novella - £100
Best Short Story - £50

Best Flash Fiction - £25
Best Poem - £25

Winners of each category will have their work published on this web page and will receive a complimentary copy of The Paul Cave Prize for Literature 2023 book to be published by the end of 2023.

All approved submissions will feature in The Paul Cave Prize for Literature 2023. Each writer who submits a piece of approved work is guaranteed to have it published in the book.

How to enter

1. email your submission(s) to tsaunderspubs@gmail.com
2. send payment by Paypal to tsaunderspubs@gmail.com

TIM SAUNDERS PUBLICATIONS
poetry, fiction and memoir

"Everybody has a book in them," according to
journalist Christopher Hitchens (1949 to 2011)

Do you have a book you would like to publish?

Email. tsaunderspubs@gmail.com

For more information visit:
tsaunderspubs.weebly.com

*Regular writing opportunities including monthly
challenges and The Paul Cave Prize for Literature*

MARY BUCHAN

Printed in Great Britain
by Amazon

27452270R00051